BUSINESS

AN INNOVATIVE APPROACH TO BUSINESS STARTUP, GROWTH AND EFFECTIVENESS

by

Tom Mahalo

presentation of the information is without the contract or any type of guarantee assurance.

The trademarks that are used are without any consent, and the publication of the trademark is without permission or backing by the trademark owner. All trademarks and brands within this book are for clarifying

purposes only and are the owned by the owners themselves, not affiliated with this document.

Contents

Introduction

First off, I would love to just say thank you for taking the time to get this book about BUSINESS. My name is Tom Mahalo, an expert of more than YEARS years' worth of planning and preparation for businesses. In this guide, you'll find the steps that I have followed for some time to make sure that any business I work within or start has been built on the soundest and the safest of foundations.

This is hard work and usually means that you have to sacrifice both a fast start and the immediacy of making money, but the long-term benefits are massive. Whether you intend on offering a physical service in your local area, selling products in one area, going online and doing you're selling or even freelancing online you'll find that the ideas in this guide can help you be a genuine success.

One of the major failings of most businesses today comes from being unable to quantify the success of your competition. Instead of seeing your competition as barriers to success, see them as springboards and examples to follow. The thought leaders and industry giants are there to be used as a guideline to success, not as something to limit success.

The other main problem that businesses' suffer from is a lack of planning in their foundations. From the reasons for their existence right through to the way that clients are treated, many businesses will fail to cover even the basics when it comes to how they work with their client. In this guide, then, you'll find all the ideas that you need to get your mind racing and putting you in the right mindset to deliver consistent success for years to come.

Something that many people make the mistake with when they run a business is the idea that they need to always be seen as the main authority and that they have to be the dominant force within their business, commanding staff like they are peasants.

Well, in this guide we'll try to break down that kind of thinking and help you see the "new" way of managing a business. We'll be calling this "Hope over Fear" and the idea is that you will be using the positivity of your products or services to make a telling difference to the opinion and the beliefs of your clients. Instead of playing on their fears to make them buy, you'll be giving them the positive side of the story to help them start to believe and understand what you actually offer.

So, across the rest of this guide we'll be breaking down the logic behind planning and the benefits of using positivity instead of negativity to control the narrative of your business. The success and failure that you will face in the years to come will come from how your business is operated and looked after by yourself and your staff as much as anything else so make sure you take this into account when you start planning!

Let's look at the first section – Starting a Business. In here. We'll detail the questions you need to ask yourself and the answers that you need to have prepared if you wish to be a success in the years to come.

Starting a Business

One of the most challenging aspects of running your own business comes from how you manage the beginning of the business. There are numerous questions that you need to find a genuine answer to, such as;

- How do you present your business?
- How will you market yourself?
- What kind of market is there for your business?
- Can you get access to products and supplies?
- Is there a local demand or do you have to expand?
- Will you start as an offline or online business?

- Do you need funding to get started?
- How much competition do you have?

With so many questions to consider and not enough time to get all of the answers, you have to consider the best way to move forward from a financial point of view. In this section, starting a Business, we'll take a closer look at the kind of answers that you might be looking for to answer each and every one of these vital questions for business startup.

How do you present your business?

This is how you will try and come across – every business needs to have a set range of parameters that it follows at all times with how it wants to come across. What's the theme? What are you trying to build?

Your business should have some kind of end-game or answer that it provides and speaks to. For example, if you were selling dietary supplements then you would wish to come across with authority and as the solution needed. Your business has to match the kind of attitude your solution provides.

How will you market yourself?

Getting marketing off the ground is perhaps a question for later on in the process but you will find that smart marketing of your business will come from how you try to come across online and/or offline. You have to look at various factors like your target market, how easily you can handle shipping to further locations and how you can get noticed in more than one place.

What kind of market is there for your business?

There are numerous markets open to you in any line of business but each industry is different. Some have different avenues to go down from selling specific products based around that to finding supplemental products and/or services that relate to that service. The market depends on your industry but should be something that you take into full consideration before going any further.

Can you get access to products and supplies?

You'll have to know before you start if you can get access to the products or services needed to make the business work. This might sound obvious, but you would be shocked at how many businesses start up and use the wrong information and don't have the correct details in place long before they get started.

Is there a local demand or do you have to expand?

Take this into account as it might answer the next question, too. If you have a catchment area that is very specific then you might be best served concentrating on offline business methods more. If you have to go a bit further afield to find clients then you might find that going online will be the most effective service for you initially.

Will you start as an offline or online business?

The same as above, but something you should always take into account. Whilst no business should concentrate on just one, you need to have a major preference to be a proper success. This will help you concentrate marketing efforts and help you really see and understand what your business requires.

Do you need funding to get started?

Are you capable of starting and just using your business from day one without any investment? Or do you need money to get premises, supplies, marketing etc. carried out?

How much competition do you have?

Look around you both on the web and locally – who is potentially standing in your way and stopping you from being a success? Taking the time to understand this will help you become far more likely to succeed in the coming years. It's a small step, but a very important one.

As you can see, there are many questions to ask yourself about starting a business. To reach the height of your potential and to avoid limiting yourself to success, you should try and answer every question. Also, you have one more major factor to take into account that will vary depending on where you are based – registering your business.

Every country is different but you should make a point of speaking to an advisor or expert on this subject within your own country – they can help you understand where you might be going wrong.

Aside from this, your business needs to know its catchment area, the potential for success, the demand for your goods or services and the viability of being able to actually sell them. After all, your business has to make sense with both what people want and the kind of services or skills that you can provide!

There is no point starting a business with no demand or one that you cannot hope to actually provide the service for. Before you go any further, make sure that you can produce a logical and cohesive answer for everything that we just addressed. Next, we're going to take a look at various things that you would do well to consider if you want to have a chance of being a successful business.

Things to Consider

Just like starting up any kind of enterprise or good idea, you will have numerous things that you will have to consider. To help you find the gist of what you may need to be a success, we recommend that you take into account the following questions. Each of them will help you, as a beginner, understand the motivations for what you intend to do and also whether or not it's going to be a viable route to go down.

Starting a business can be a really scary prospect, but it's made much easier if you consider;

Do I Have The Skills?

Everyone goes into their line of work and their business beginning thinking they offer something new and fresh to the industry – but do you?

Take the time out to go and view your competition, and we don't just mean a brief look into their website. Get involved with the business and go as far as you can without actually using their service (if you can afford to then you should 100% use it, though) as this will give you a good idea of who you're up against. This is not only a great way to scope out the competition but it might give you an idea of just how far above/behind the curve you are at this moment in time.

Another reason to do this is because it will let you see how good you are at doing something that many people don't consider as part of the job – selling. Let's say you are opening up a business which sells cars – you might be able to get quality cars and provide them at good prices, but can you sell them? If you lack the skills to sell as well as do the job, you might need some assistance.

Do You Want to Run A Business?

This is a question that you no doubt go "Yeah, obviously!" too but a lot of people think they want to run a business. Let's say that you love fixing and building computers. Well, instead of running a business that does this you should just find an employment position that does this – running a business means that you need to have a desire to do the job **and** handle all the madness that comes with being the owner of a business. It takes more than the skill itself to succeed.

One of the most important factors to take into account here is the fact that your business will need to be run by you, so you have to be prepared to do more than just the basic service. You have to handle customers, set up supplies, manage books, run the shop and the website, build it all up, deal with marketing, handle complaints, think up new stock and then get somewhere to store it. And that's just the very beginning!

This is the most important thing to consider – do you have the heart to handle everything that comes with business?

Many people only want the former, but they hate the idea of having the latter.

The core of any good business is built around someone who can do both; if you are unable to commit to being as good at administration, team building, financial management and business preparation as you are at the primary skills needed, take a step back. It's always best to delay the opening of a business until the answer to this question is crystal clear.

Decide on this before you begin, and you can save years of debt, stress, failure and frustration from holding you back.

However, don't let this part put you off the idea of running a business – you can outsource most of the ideas we are talking about. This just means that you need to have the funds and the contacts to get someone who is an expert in each of these fields to take on the responsibility. In short, running a business will ask of you one major question you need to make sure you have the right answer for – can you afford to pay someone else to run it for you? Or do you have the time to learn how to do it all on your own?

Can You Let Go?

The last major question you need to answer is this – are you capable of letting go? You might have a dream of just working away in your workshop doing whatever it is that you intend to do for a living, but one day – if you are a success – you'll have to delegate. As time goes on and success becomes a major factor of your business you will have to quite quickly accept that you have to become more owner, less worker. Instead of doing the job, you'll be hiring delegates to do it all for you.

Business ownership changes the parameters of your success and this is the time that many people fail or don't like the future they see. Instead of just going along with the old job of doing the service and providing it from your small business, you'll soon have to be the one who manages the administration or at the very least manages the management!

This means leaving behind your dream of just doing what you are passionate about for a living all day – if you really crave to do just that, employment is better suited.

Getting Experience

It's very important to have some genuine experience within the industry you want to work within, so if you wish to open a business in any industry you should work in it first. Take six months to go and work within the industry. If you wished to run a clothes store you would look for a job in one, if you wished to run a restaurant then you would open up a restaurant and see what you think from here.

This can help you open your eyes and see the immense opportunity, as well as the challenges, involved. Ask some questions of your manager and see what they think and how they respond.

With all this said, then, you can hopefully understand the major challenges which are at play when you just start to run a business. There is more to consider than just what we covered in the first section, so be sure to take all of this into account.

Are you still sure this is what you wish to do? Then let's take an innovate look at how you can start growing your business – any business – from the ground up. Everything we look at should be actionable and affordable, so long as you are committed to the time and effort needed.

Growing your Business

The world of business today, thanks to the advent of the internet, has changed forever. Gone are the days of small local brands that control the community – welcome to the free market, where everyone can advertise anywhere. Many of the products you buy and use today will come from nowhere near where you live and for you, this should be the goal. You might have dreamt of a small local workshop but thinking small brings limitations that you'll likely never grow out of and could hamper the future of your business – instead, growing your business should always be about thinking big.

In this section, we'll take a look at some great ideas that you can use to grow your business whether you are online or offline, selling services or products. Each suggestion can be used to help you establish yourself and also ensure you don't get lost in the challenge of being a modern day business owner.

Growing your business successfully means that you will need to be capable of;

Showcasing your own passion for the subject. When someone comes to see you about the service or products you offer – or even visits your website – they need to be able to really feel that authenticity and passion emitting from you. Selling is all about being enthusiastic, so if you are struggling with the art of selling you merely need to think of all the good things that your business will bring to the table for every potential customer! Passion is the most powerful tool you have for consistent growth.

Also, you have to be able to get involved. As your business goes and you likely go from being a sole operator with freelance help to operating with a staff, you have to be a leader. However, being a leader is more than man management and keeping everyone laughing – it's about making sure you set the example. When things are tough and business is struggling, or even when you are overwhelmed, it pays to be able to get your sleeves rolled up and join in yourself. Staff and clients alike want to see the business owner getting involved in the job!

Handling all of the “little” tasks. You should never be afraid to get your hands dirty to lead by example as it shows to your clients and staff that you don’t feel as if you are above the job. Besides, every little adjustment and change can be seen to help.

Focusing on the customer. Any good business is capable of handling their customers’ demands and helping them understand why they need what you offer or sell. It’s easy to create a customer, but creating a happy one is much harder. A happy customer will come back in the future, spread your name across the town – maybe even the world – and be sure to give people a positive response about the service that you offer. Never be afraid to put the customer first, even at the expense of short-term profitability; long-term growth is going to be far more important for you.

Being competitive. Another significant factor in your development and growth as a business will be from your ability to accept completion. This means offering a competitive and unique advantage over your clients – you need to come with a strong, effective sales proposition. Your unique sales point is all about making sure you can offer something more than the competition, so make sure that your business is always going to be looking for that point so that you can hammer it down. When customers think of your business, they need to have one major point that sticks – so create one!

Managing your economy. A good business today is capable of looking after the money that it has to ensure that long-term growth can happen. Aside from the very earliest days of your business you should never be running at a deficit. You should be focusing on the best ways to enhance and grow your profit streams up so that you have a long-term sustainability goal. Remember, you want to focus on your net profit not the gross profit. Understand the limitations that you have financially so that you can grow to add these features and systems without falling into major debt. Another major factor of managing your economic situation can come from a reading of any training modules from Robert Kiyosaki. He's brilliant about detailing the financial situation of the world, and how you can adapt to fit with the ever changing parameters which the financial world has set to success.

Measuring your success. No business just automatically hits its goal and aims, you have to be able to make sure you have analysis and measurement to follow this. From website analytics to let you know your visitor numbers to using sales staff to give you an idea of how well your best products are doing, you need to have a strong and clear idea of where your business is going. By this, we simply mean that you are ready to accept that your growth will come as a point of reaching these targets, not the other way around.

Lastly, always try and concentrate on being the best business that you can. This might sound obvious but self-improvement and striving for change can become a major issue once you first taste success. Never think that you know everything about your industry, and you'll find it easier to become the leader.

Hitting the Ground Running

One of the most effective ways for you to start making a progressive change to the way that you work is to get some genuine leadership and business training. Whether you turn to someone like Tony Robins or Brian Tracy, you'll find the cost of training more than worth your time. Leadership training can help you avoid getting into a pickle and finding yourself over your head in dealing with some of the trickier parts of being involved in running a business.

Another good way to build your confidence and your belief is to do a spot of public speaking. This can help you really capitalize on your knowledge and pass it on to others – it also lets you build your belief in yourself. Most importantly, though, it helps you get noticed which can play a significant role in helping you develop your plan for the future.

Having an inspirational person to look up to and follow in terms of how you act and deal with situations is another major benefit that you can really benefit from having. Not only will this give you far more control over the direction that you are heading in as a business owner but it will help you see a strong example of what works – and, of course, what doesn't!

Another recommendation would be that you pick up some reading materials on business management and motivation. These will help you avoid falling off the cliff when the difficulty level you face spikes and you find yourself dealing with a feeling of not knowing here to go. Doing this will help you become far more attuned with your own thinking and where you are headed as a professional. Most importantly, though, it avoids major mess-ups by following the wrong kind of example!

As you can see, there are major challenges associated with being a strong business which shows the signs of growth, development and stability which is needed. If you wish to make sure you are getting into this situation as quickly as you can then we recommend that you take into account all of the above.

They will ensure that your business has strong groundings which help it stay competitive and capable of being a success.

More importantly they will make sure you don't over commit to any one section of your project. Remember, running a business locally might be the aim today but that aim will have to change if you have any true and genuine ambitions about growing your business.

Next, let's take a look at how you can capitalize and then build upon this growth to ensure your long-term future.

Building your Business

Once you understand the principles of why you run your business and how you can make it grow, you now have to understand how to lay the right foundations. It's important to be ambitious, to put the customer first and to always have the best possible methods to bring your business forward into the future. However, it's also equally important to make sure that the very philosophy and foundation of your business is right.

If you take any kind of interest in professional sports, you're probably sick of hearing the word 'philosophy' as it seems to be the go-to card for a struggling coach. However, taking away the mindless middle-management side of building a business and having a philosophy, it's the most important and vital factor to your continued success.

So, what are the most important elements in a business which manages to maintain its growth?

What signs are needed?

Creating a Concept

You need to have a genuine concept in place long before you start building anything. We've spoken so far about the importance of being competitive and putting the right building blocks in place, but there is FAR more to building your business than just that. You first have to dedicate the time and money needed to building a clear concept – this is the very parameters around who you hire, what you sell, and why you're open in the first place.

Take yourself into the mind of the customer and think what your business aims to achieve – this is your concept. How you go about forging and strengthening that concept will almost entirely decide how likely you are to be a success in the future. The business concept that you want to build upon should be an image that is for the customer – what is the #1 problem you wish to solve?

Finding Your Market

Next, you have to understand what your business stands for within the market you are in. start doing some serious market research as you go – speak to people who would fall into your potential demographic. Let's say that you are running a company which sells smart phone apps that help people look after their college coursework.

It's a simple idea but it will typically have a very specific catchment area. You then need to analyze the kind of people you would likely be targeting, making sure that when you describe the idea that they just what you are talking about. If they don't, then the idea has to be refined and simplified – the concept and standing for your business has to be something that your target demographic will notice and recognize instantly.

Place your Foundations

Now that you have a concept and a demographic to target, you have to start putting in place the foundations to attract these people. If you are running the app business above then you want to get on your website, your social media channels and even web forums to start creating a buzz for your product. Online marketing will be the backbone of your success and your very foundations. However, if you were to run a local pet management service then you would probably go for local social media channels and advertising through community centers, leaflet posting and even advertising in related store windows.

No business has the same foundations as the next – to be a success and to build your business beyond those initial growth levels you have to consider that moving forward. Set in place your foundations for marketing and targeting the kind of people that fit into the framework and concept for the business you own.

Stay Educated

Another major element to your success will come from how well you educate yourself on the matters that are going to dictate your success. By this we mean a rather simple approach to staying involved with the most effective ways to run your own specific kind of business.

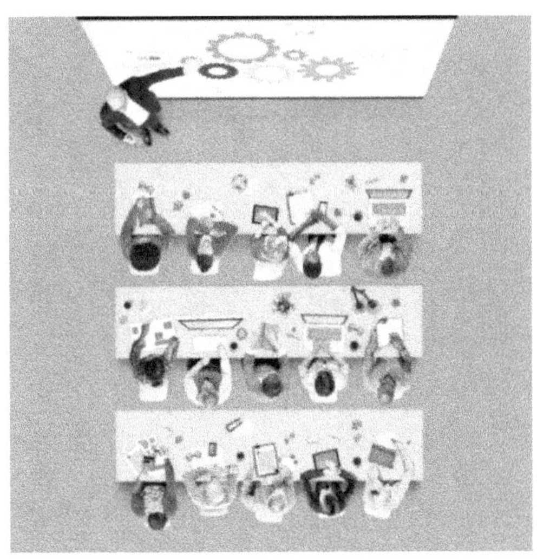

It can help you overcome the major issue of being a worker, not a seller that we spoke of earlier. More importantly, though, it helps you stay ahead of the curve. As your business grows and time passes the industry you work in will change incredibly and you need to be ready to change with it. This is why reading into and adapting to fit with all of the most important industry factors and changes will play such a significant factor in your chances of being a success.

Always staying educated and up-to-date with the latest goings on within your industry will play a critical role in the level of development that you expect to see occur in the long-term. Sure, it might take a bit of patience to put this in place but it is by no means impossible.

By taking the time to stay educated you build your business by learning new tricks. You can shave off months of development and thousands of dollars wasted in experiments simply by educating yourself!

Start Networking

As your business builds and expands you will have to make friends. Whether that is befriending suppliers to get better rates in the long-term to becoming friends with people who will publish and sell your products for you, networking is a major element to being a success as a business.

To build a business, though, you have to accept that starting networking means more than just getting yourself a better deal.

It might mean having to offer a better deal yourself to get that person or group involved.

Even if you have no stock and only sell online, befriending the press & bloggers, for example, can help you get more exposure. Building a business is all about that exposure so making sure that you can get it is a major factor in being a success.

This is all about successful growth, so how do you take those first steps to success?

Your First Steps

Now you know what your business needs to succeed and what your business has to understand to first grow and then build upon that growth, how do you take your first steps to making this actionable?

It's all well and good knowing how to go about doing all of this and working with it on your own, but you have to accept that changes will need to be made along the way. The first steps that you should be taking towards your success, though, should be built around discovering the answer to one major, constantly recurring question;

"Can I do this all on my own?"

This keeps people up at night – can they run the business themselves? It all depends on the line of work that you intend to run. Let's say that your business is a service that provides website design and content management for businesses – you can do all of this on your own, with the right teaching and enough time.

However, if you are getting involved in a service that is going to sell bespoke car parts, for example, you'll need other services to assist you. Your first steps towards taking on that growth and building on it, then, should be built around understanding if you are capable of doing it all on your own.

The most major factor that comes into play here when building your business, then, starts with knowing if you can provide everything from start to finish without professional input.

Knowing your Limits

The first thing to think about, then, is how good you are at any given task. Are you capable of managing or handling something more than your skills? We spoke earlier about how you could outsource the parts of running a business that you cannot do. So long as you have the money to cover that then its fine, because it's vital to know your limits. It's equally as damaging to just ignore parts of your business like administration and networking than it is to do them poorly due to a lack of experience on your end.

Therefore, you can actually save money in the long-term by hiring an expert to deal with the sections of running a business that you can't. Knowing if you can do things on your own or if you need help will ensure you get plenty of help when you're moving forward.

Arranging the Finance

Any good business plan today is built upon a strong financial footing. If you have to hire in help then you should have several months of salary for each person ready to go and be paid out. The vital services your business needs to have success – again, changing entirely depending on your industry and business type – have to be thoroughly researched and costed. Again, look to the competition in your market and see how they handle this part of the business.

Are they dealing with it all themselves? Or are they bringing in some third party experts to handle the service?

The vast majority will need at least some help to make sure you can succeed. For any new business that wants a strong marketing platform you'll either need finances for;

An offline business – marketing leaflets, design for the leaflets, people to send the leaflets out, direct mailing costs, advertising costs in local media.

An online business – website designer, website marketing team, social media management group, graphical designer, content writer.

Thankfully, all of these can be outsourced and found so long as you have the finance to pay for them. Taking the first steps to being a strong business, though, comes from knowing that you have the right people you can trust to help you get to spread the word about what you offer.

If you are ready to start a business then you will already have the skills needed to do the actual service you offer or to create/source the products you sell, but you need to have people to help get you noticed. This is especially important if you are still working on becoming a natural seller yourself, so it helps to have people there – and the money – to actually pay for it in the long-term!

One of the most important factors in being a success as a business owner, then comes from being able to see that these first steps towards being noticed will require you to handle lots of side-projects that have to be costed, and more than likely have to be outsourced.

The "Boring" Details

Another major factor to consider for any business, both online and/or offline, comes from how you handle the important stuff. From creating a business with the government so that you have official records to getting staff payrolls, accounts and even an official logo created all takes time, effort and money.

You will need to accept quite quickly that the first steps to making your business a strong part of the industry you wish to break into will require you to work exceptionally hard at creating the right atmosphere which will foster an attitude of success amongst every member.

The boring details, though, have to be made as part of your growth and building. You don't want to spend all of that time building your business and marketing it when you have no official right to be a business at that moment in time, so be sure to handle all of the official details as early on in your tenure as you possibly can.

The last significant factor to take into account regarding taking your first steps will involve helping you understand the importance of managing the financial side of things. From getting the money together to get experts involved to hiring people to just handle the basics for you, the opening steps to any successful business today will come not just from your own input, but the input of the people that you hire.

To do this successfully you need to set goals – but how do you decide what goals to go for?

Setting your Goals

For any business to be a success, it needs to have smart and actionable goals. Whilst your goals should always to be profitable and always growing, your goals have to be a bit more specific than that. After all, that's the aim of any business!

So, when it comes to setting your goals, how do you think you should operate? What comes across as the most effective way for you to start managing, preparing and looking after the long-term future of your business?

Every business is different, of course, but we recommend that you take into consideration the following;

Work Incrementally

Make sure that your goals are nice and specific – this might sound obvious but it's very easy to set ambiguous goals that you simply cannot achieve. This is done quite easily and to avoid it you need to consider the fact that your goals match the industry and the realistic nature of your business.

Many businesses can set targets that were never attainable in the first place, and then can quite disheartened when they find out that this the target was never even close to being achieved.

Make sure that any goals that you set are provided with a clear and obvious end-game; and make sure that your goals are changing incrementally. By this we mean make sure that if you wanted to have 25 new clients last month, you only want to have 30-35 new ones this month; never expect too much, and grow organically.

Go Public

Make sure that all goals you set are made in public. This might seem a bit odd but it really does help to set the tone for what you want to make possible. Get at least one more member of your business – or even a close confidant at the start – to make sure they know what your goals are going to be.

If you keep your goals to yourself then you will never have any accountability.

So long as someone knows that you have a genuine plan to follow it makes it much easier for them to help you stay on target and to reach the kind of goals that you had set out from the start. Everything that you will learn from doing this will ensure you never have an excuse to fall behind or to move the goalposts – public goals are much harder to avoid sticking to!

Setting Deadlines

Set deadlines for all goals – goals with no deadline can become open-ended and thus completed. Be sure to look at your goals because they have to come with a genuine plan to go along with – goals without a deadline lacks commitment and a genuine reasoning for its existing in the place.

Choose a date that fits with the realism of what you are asking for and it will make it much easier for you to reach that goal. More importantly it will give you an easy way to stay on course whilst maintaining your hunger to complete the goal in time.

Have an End-Game

Make sure that all of your goals are built around being a quantifiable end-game. This is another obvious factor but you would be surprised how easy it is to disregard this. Make sure you know exactly what you wish to accomplish before you start and you will find that it's something with a genuine upside should you achieve it.

Think about how you would help to set the goals for a similar business if you were asked to give advice – what seems to be the most common parameters for success and/or failure within the confines and success that you're having today?

Be Specific

Be clear about a goal and what it means for you and it will be more likely to actually be achieved. For example if you want to have a certain number of staff then you want to make it financially affordable for the business within, say, two years' time.

It's a tangible goal that has a genuine reason and an end-game, and so long as you can always remind yourself of the positive upside of sticking to this you will have a far greater chance of being a success later. Do this, and you'll find that life is much simpler!

Setting Goals Ethically

Goals aren't just about setting milestones to show everyone how good your business is, either. You have to understand that your business is supposed to be about success – so reward yourself when you reach your goals. This makes it much easier for you to stay on track with your goals and make your targets because you have two ambitions.

You not only will see your business grow which always feels good, but you know you'll have the reward waiting for you in the form of X. if you don't need incentives for yourself, then set them for the team instead.

Speak with an Expert

To learn about setting goals properly you should go and see an expert in business management about this. You'll find that this will help you find a much greater way of seeing your business from a new perspective. Speaking to a business start-up expert in a consultation can help you perhaps see other sides of your industry that you never considered.

Be sure that you work with someone who knows about setting – and succeeding with – goals. This will ensure that your business can maintain a powerful vision and never lose the clarity to make key decisions when they will make a positive impact.

Now you know about how to set your goals, how do you make sure that you are on target with those goals? You have to arrange them in the right order. Prioritize what should come first – typically, you want to make sure that have the following areas covered;

Your business is profitable and can run itself without third party financial input.

Your business has a stable of useful staff that you can trust, even freelancers.

You can afford a poor month and can handle performance peaking and dropping.

Your business has a genuine plan to help you break into a larger market in the years to come.

You have the potential to bring customers back time and time again.

Arranging your goals and making sure they help you hit all four goals in the right order (the first being most important) is going to be a make-or-break factor for years to come. Not sure what direction to go in here? Then we recommend that you consider the next section specifically.

We'll be taking a look at how you can work towards creating a workplace atmosphere that can help everyone fall into line and feel utterly comfortable within the group.

Creating an Atmosphere

One of the most powerful factors in any business wishing to be a genuine success today will come from creating the right atmosphere.

The atmosphere within a business – online or offline – is going to be a major player in your ability to be a long-term concern within the industry of your choosing. Without the right atmosphere, even the most well-meaning and structured of businesses will fail.

The simple reason for this is that the world of business is changing – the politics of fear and buying the emotions of people through scaring them is dead, gone forever. What we have to look forward to from now on is creating an atmosphere which instead promotes ambition and excitement. People are less likely to find your business a viable concern if they can only see the negatives of the situation.

Selling the solution, not the problem, is the key to being a success in any industry. If you are supposed to be the solution then you have to be the one who promotes the positive nature of finding that solution, not the negativity of having the problem.

A Universal System

Whether you are selling information products or plastering walls, you'll find that creating an atmosphere is going to be vital to being a success. The atmosphere should rub off on you, your staff and your clients;

You should be the one who can raise morale and keep everyone else on the right path to success. If you work purely on your own then you have to be the one who keeps yourself busy and motivated, handling client concerns.

Staff have to be considered as a happy staff is a successful one. They need to be clear about the ambitions of the business and they also need to feel valued and appreciated by you. Make sure that your business is built on a culture of teamwork and rewarding success with both financial and other personal bonuses awaiting the best.

Treating Clients Properly

Another huge factor is, obviously, the clients. Good clients for your business atmosphere are those who understand the kind of solutions that you offer and are genuinely interested in being a part of those solutions. If you can create an atmosphere that shows clients the benefits of working with you instead of the downsides of not doing so, you'll be promoting hope over fear.

In the modern business world, hope trumps fear every time.

This makes a MAJOR difference in the long-term growth and change of your business. When people can see that you offer a more positive and progressive approach instead of telling them all about the big bad nature of what happens without you (hope over fear) then your chances of being picked are going to improve.

Hope over Fear

Most importantly, though, most of your competition will likely be promoting using fear still. Not enough businesses, new and old, are promoting using hope. For this purpose, then, you should be concentrating on creating company goals and business aims which are based upon creative hope for clients, not indulging and eating their fear!

You can break the mold and get clients interested almost immediately by just giving them a taste of what a positive business within the industry you operate within can offer. All of your promotional tools, all of your staff meetings and your entire business philosophy should be built around helping people through offering the best service possible.

If your business goals are built around trying to make people scared to try and get them to buy in, you are already failing.

Any business worth working with today is going to be far more at home promoting through the language of comfort, peace and promotion. Regardless of what you sell or offer and no matter what the niche is, the most powerful weapon that you can possibly have by your side here is going to be the ability to create the right atmosphere.

Creating the Atmosphere

When it comes to setting your goals, then, you should always be taking into account the atmosphere you want to set. The atmosphere dictates how goals are operated on so if you can create an atmosphere that brings everyone together, promotes free exchange of opinion and beliefs and never stifles personal creativity and initiative, you'll be far more likely to succeed.

If you have done any kind of reading into the old model of running a business you'll see that it's all about setting harsh targets and punishing those who fail to get there. However, a business with happy and loyal staff tends to be the most successful one so if you can make an incentive within your business from day one then success is only just around the corner if you are willing to work for it!

Rewarding Success

One of the most effective and useful parts of creating an atmosphere is to reward your staff. Take the time to create an incentives program that keeps them happy and committed to maintaining the message you have set, and goals are far more likely to be achieved.

Remember, the best goals are going to be built around the new model of hope over fear. A business which operates on positivity will inspire others to be positive whether you are looking at the way that your clients look at your business or how your staff properly represent you.

With all of this in mind, then, how do you maintain a level of consistency within the atmosphere of your business? We'll be taking a look at how you do this from a management perspective. This will assume that you have other members of staff operating alongside you, but even if you are working solo you should find that it's relatively easy to understand how all of this can happen.

From arranging a strong company policy from day one to giving staff freedom to express their concerns and excitement, managing consistency within a new business in the modern era can be tough work – so let's find out how!

Maintaining Consistency

When you build a business with sound foundations and you have created a method for it to advertise within your geographical and logistical limitations, you are well on the way to success. Likewise, when you set goals and arrange an atmosphere that promotes positive thinking, group engagement and people getting involved you'll see an incredible jump in productivity.

However, even the fastest starts for a business can never last – something will always affect your chances of being successful. So, how do you counter and prepare for these problems in the workplace or with clients?

With Staff

When managing a group of staff you have to be prepared for debate and arguments, even in a positively driven environment. Ego and the desire for success will eventually put people against one another and it's up to you then, as business leader, to find the cause for this situation. It will take some time and it will require you to work hard and be prepared to study the inner psychology of group management a bit further but it's certainly not impossible.

Maintaining your consistency is going to be a key factor in how successful your business is going to be for the years to come. The most effective way to plan for all of this, then, is to create a forum that allows everyone to speak openly with each other. It's always best to have problems dealt with and understood by staff as then everyone can air their thoughts and create a more positive forum for discussion later on down the line.

Being able to work with your staff in a position that lets them express themselves is so exceptionally important for the long-term. Make sure that to maintain your business practices that you give every staff member to both personal goals they need to meet and the long-term company goals. This lets everyone see the bigger picture and should stop things like ego taking over.

You want staff to be passionate and caring about their work without ever compromising the capability of everyone else to be a success within the company framework too. Worried that this won't be the case? Then arrange consultations on a monthly/bi-monthly basis with all of your staff members to air any grievances with you.

As the owner of the business you hold the utmost accountability for all success – and all failure. Therefore to maintain consistency you should make it easy for staff to come forward with any problems they have either to you or the colleague that they are having problems with. Most modern businesses struggle when opening the floor to their staff; don't make the same mistake and instead allow clear and open expression of ideas to be a major part of the way that you work on a daily basis.

Staff can even help you point out flaws in the long-term plan! Try and reward staff for strong performance levels, too. It can help keep them motivated and engaged for the business' success.

With Clients

When it comes to helping out a client you should accept that it's far harder – they don't need your business to make a living. Instead clients have to be someone who needs you specifically and is happy to work with you. Making this the consistent answer that you get back is hugely difficult, but it is by no means an impossibility so long as you are willing to work at it and set the tone with every single client.

Create a process with your staff – or on your own if you work individually in your new business – that ensures clients can always voice their positives and negatives. It's something that will genuinely give you all the help that you need in forging a long-term future for yourself for years to come.

Clients appreciate it when they are given a chance to voice their concerns to a member of staff personally so make sure this option is always open. Make the communication that clients have with your business as clear as possible and they should have no problem understanding your consistency when addressed.

With clients, you always want to be delivering a service that suits them anyway but the success of your business is literally founded upon the development, growth and happiness of your client list. With that in mind, you should do everything you can to keep them on-side; this includes offering some kind of client reward scheme.

From a loyalty program to a system that makes sure clients always feel as if they are being heard, you can make it much easier for clients to trust in the kind of message that your business is actively promoting at this moment in time.

To do this properly, make sure that your business undertakes a performance exam with every client. Every client should be handed a form –

electronically or otherwise – that allows them to evaluate your performance and send it back to you.

This will quickly help you understand the most important elements of your chances of being a success. With client feedback you'll see where the discrepancies in performance are coming from and how you can avoid this later.

So, now you know what could inhibit – or improve – performance, what matters will you take to enforce this for your business?

Conclusion

There you have it – we hope that you have enjoyed reading this guide. Everything included in here has been built over many years of experience and knowledge of starting businesses in numerous industries and guises. From websites that sell products for health to businesses that offer manual labor skills, we make sure everything that has been offered in here is easy to be a part of and understand.

One thing that really caught our attention when writing this guide, though, was the fact that most businesses we dealt with when creating this were starting to really make an impact. We've helped numerous startup companies make a success of themselves by helping them understand the importance of business ideas that are built upon long-term sustainability.

Now, you can hopefully see that a strong and effective business today is built upon the foundations of offering truth and honesty over anything else. Your clients will want to know everything about your service and what you can offer so it makes perfect sense to come up with a plan that caters to this!

By following the advice in this guide you should be able to understand the major factors that help a business move from being “a” choice to “the” choice. There is a major difference, and it usually comes in the way that your business operates.

If your business has strong goals, understands its industry and respects its clients then your chances of success are being massively improved with every passing day. More importantly, though, it helps you understand that your business is going to be a long-term aim.

Unless you literally offer something that is re-inventing the wheel then it will take a period of time to get above your opposition and become a more refined business for years to come.

By taking into account the fact that your business should be a devotion of months and years of hard work, you'll become far more capable of being a genuine success down the line. Your business should be built on sound foundations, foundations that capture the aim and the goals that you have set for your future and the future of your industry.

Remember to stay positive, to set actionable goals and – most importantly – to stay in touch with the idea of creating hope for clients instead of playing on their fears. Reward clients and staff alike for loyalty and performance, too, and your business will have the greatest chance that it has ever had to be a success.

From a painter to a piper, any business today can thrive from following the steps set forward in this book. Set goals, retain your ideas for treating everyone with respect and decorum, and give your staff the ability and space needed to just be themselves and success really is not too far away.

Best of luck!

Tom Mahalo

www.ingramcontent.com/pod-product-compliance
Lightning Source LLC
Chambersburg PA
CBHW060409190526
45169CB00002B/817

* 9 7 8 1 5 3 3 0 5 2 3 4 6 *